I0233918

UNDER WESTERN EYES

Borgo Press Dramas by FRANK J. MORLOCK

Chuzzlewit
Crime and Punishment
Falstaff (with William Shakespeare, John Dennis, and William Kendrick)
Fathers and Sons
The Idiot
Justine
The Marquis de Sade (with Charles Méré)
Notes from the Underground
Outrageous Women: Lady Macbeth and Other French Plays (editor and translator)
Peter and Alexis
The Princess Casamassima
A Raw Youth
The Stendhal Hamlet Scenarios and Other Shakespearean Shorts from the French (editor and translator)
Under Western Eyes

UNDER WESTERN EYES

A PLAY IN THREE ACTS

FRANK J. MORLOCK

Adapted from the Novel by Joseph Conrad

THE BORGO PRESS
MMXII

UNDER WESTERN EYES

Copyright © 2012 by Frank J. Morlock

FIRST EDITION

Published by Wildside Press LLC

www.wildsidebooks.com

DEDICATION

For Milan Jurecka

CONTENTS

CAST OF CHARACTERS. 9

ACT I, Scene 1 11

ACT I, Scene 2 21

ACT I, Scene 3 37

ACT II, Scene 4. 49

ACT II, Scene 5. 65

ACT III, Scene 6 93

ACT III, Scene 7 107

EPILOGUE, Scene 8 123

ABOUT THE AUTHOR 129

CAST OF CHARACTERS

Haldin

Razumov

The Prince

General Tulayev

Peter Ivanovitch

N. N.

Yakovlitch (who does not speak)

Nathalie Haldin

Eleanor Maximovna

Sophia Antonovna

Seven men, three women

Time: After the Revolution of 1905.

ACT I

SCENE 1

A small but tidy student's room belonging to Razumov, about the turn of the century.

There is a desk, lots of books, and a bed. Razumov is a serious student. He is working over some papers, when Haldin, also a student, enters after a knock.

Razumov (looking up from his work)

Haldin—is that you? This is indeed unexpected. Come, sit down and have a smoke.

Haldin (nervously)

Are you busy? Am I interrupting you?

Razumov

Well, I've set my heart on the silver medal, and I was about to tackle the essay.

Haldin

Very commendable. Your diligence is known throughout the university.

Razumov

It's nice of you to say so.

Haldin

Kirylo Sidorovitch, we are not exactly in the same camp. Your judgment is more philosophical than mine. You are a man of few words—but I haven't met any one, no not one student, who doubted the generosity of your sentiments.

Razumov

I'm flattered.

Haldin

You are solid—and solidity like that cannot exist without character. You do not throw your soul to the winds. Your reserve has always fascinated me. So, I tried to remember your address. It was a wonderful piece of luck. I remembered correctly. I met no one on the stairs—not a soul.

Razumov

Well, I'm delighted you came to see me. It's terrible weather, and I could use a visit. I'm reserved, but I'm not really unfriendly.

Haldin

It happened I was near your apartment, and I wanted to talk with you about the events that occurred this morning.

Razumov

Ah, you mean the assassination of the Minister of the Interior? Yes, everyone's talking about it. An astounding event.

Haldin (calmly)

It was I who removed that august civil servant this morning.

(Pause.)

Razumov (aside)

There goes my silver medal.

Haldin

You say nothing! I understand your silence. To be sure,

I cannot expect you, with your frigid English manners, to embrace me. But, you know what that man was doing. He had to be stopped—and I, I stopped him. Yes, brother, I killed him. Still, it's weary work. True, the man was a maniac, but it is a pity to have to kill anyone. But anyone who can declare solemnly that, "The thought of liberty never existed in God's mind," has to be removed from office one way or another.

Razumov (slowly)

How did it happen? All I heard was that he had been killed in broad daylight.

Haldin

He was driving to his office in his sleigh. We've had knowledge of his movements for some time. The Central Committee appointed Markov and myself to dispatch him— I haven't slept for ten days— Anyway, Markov threw the first bomb. It killed the driver, but the Minister was unharmed. A crowd formed, of course. I was posted further down the street. When I saw what had happened, I came up behind the crowd and lobbed my bomb over their heads. That finished him.

Razumov

And you got away?

Haldin

As you see. I certainly didn't expect to. When the bomb went off, everyone started running, and I was no more conspicuous than anyone else. Actually, it was so easy, I couldn't believe it.

Razumov

But, why come to me? Certainly you had made plans to escape.

Haldin

Of course, of course. I went to Ziemianitch. He is a peasant who keeps horses for hire. Unfortunately, he was not there, and so, I thought it better not to arouse suspicion by staying around. So, here I am.

Razumov

But, pardon me, Victor Victorovitch, we barely know each other. I don't see why you—

Haldin

Confidence.

Razumov

In me?

Haldin

I told you. You are much respected. We know your heart is in the right place.

Razumov

It seems I have a reputation I wasn't aware of.

Haldin

I am not a destroyer. The true destroyers are those who destroy the human spirit. Men like me are necessary to make room for self contained, thinking men like you. Well, we have prepared for the sacrifice of our lives. But, since I have come off so well, I want to escape if it can be done. It is not my life I want to save, but my powers to act: I won't live idle. Oh, no! Don't make any mistake, Razumov, men like me are rare. Besides, my escape will drive the police frantic—not to mention the Tsar.

Razumov

What do you want me to do?

Haldin

Help me to vanish.

Razumov

You want to stay here?

Haldin

Only for a short time. No great risk in that as no one has seen me come. Go and see Ziemianitch for me.

Razumov

What am I to tell him?

Haldin

Tell him, "Kolya will meet you half an hour after midnight, at the seventh lamppost counting from the upper end of Kesabelnaya Street."

Razumov

Are you certain you were seen by no one when you came here?

Haldin

I'm as sure as I can be. I waited for two hours before coming up.

Razumov

Still, you're a noticeable person— Yes—of course, I

will go. You must give me precise instructions, and for the rest—depend on me.

Haldin (embracing him)

I knew I could count on you. You're collected, cool, a regular Englishman. There aren't many like you. Look here, brother: Men like me leave no posterity—but their souls are not lost. No man's soul is ever lost. It works for itself, or else where would be the sense of self sacrifice, of martyrdom? Don't misunderstand, Razumov. What I did today was not murder—it was war. My spirit shall go on warring in some Russian body until all falsehood is swept out of the world. (Razumov remains silent throughout this harangue) Ha, you say nothing—you are a skeptic! I respect your philosophical skepticism—but I don't touch the soul. The Russian soul has a mission, I tell you—or else why should I have done this like a butcher—I, I—who wouldn't hurt a fly.

Razumov

Not so loud!

(Haldin bursts into tears.)

Razumov

Try to control yourself.

Haldin

Yes, men like me have no posterity. I have a sister, though. Not a bad little girl, my sister. She will marry soon, I hope. Look at me: my father was a government official.— A true Russian in his way. But, I am not like him. More like my grandfather—a Decembrist. They shot him in Twenty-Eight. This is war, but God of Justice! It's weary work.

Razumov

You believe in God, Haldin?

Haldin

What does it matter? When your day comes, you don't forget what's divine in our Russian soul. Respect it! I am speaking to you now like a man with a rope around his neck. Don't spoil its message to the world!— I am one of the doomed. When the necessity of this heavy work came to me, and I understood it really had to be done—I said "God's will be done." That's all.

(Haldin stretches out silently on Razumov's bed.)

Razumov (after a pause)

Heldin?

Haldin

Yes?

Razumov

Hadn't I better start?

Haldin

Yes, brother. The time has come to put your faith to the test.

Razumov (displaying a key)

I am going to lock you in.

Haldin

Go with God.

BLACKOUT

ACT I
SCENE 2

A room in the palace of Prince K.

Prince K is an old man, but of a passionate, kindly disposition. He is speaking with General Tulayev, an officer in the Secret Police, a cold, somewhat analytical man. The General wears no uniform.

General

This story is hard to believe! My dear Prince—

Prince

General Tulayev, I swear to you, we have got him, this assassin.

General

Pardon my skepticism, but this is not the way one usually solves these crimes. I have been in the secret police a long time, and one doesn't usually have these things delivered in a package, so to speak.

Prince

This worthy young man came to me, and I came to you.

General

But, that's rather remarkable, his coming to you.

Prince

Why is it remarkable?

General

How had this mister—Razumov, I believe you said, come to make your acquaintance?

Prince

Mr. Razumov—is a most honorable young man, whom Providence itself—

General

To be sure, to be sure. But, this Razumov is a mere student, and you are one of the most highly placed nobles in all Russia.

Prince

I—

General

I don't mean to pry, but why did he turn to you?

Prince (flushing)

It's rather embarrassing. When I was a young man, I was rather wild, you see.

General (smiling)

A wild oat, eh?

Prince

So he is—yes?

General

So he is your son?

Prince

By a peasant girl. My first love, in fact. I still think of her. She died when he was born, poor thing.

General

And, he knows you?

Prince

He only met me recently for the first time. It was quite by accident. I was at my attorney's office, and by chance, he came about his allowance. He had no idea who his benefactor was. I had just heard such good reports of—he's quite a scholar, you know.

General

Indeed?

Prince

I was quite proud. He's very handsome, a perfect gentleman. I had never taken any interest in him before, but when I saw what a fine boy I had turned out—ah, it's all nonsense.

General

So he turned to you?

Prince

He can't very well go to some police official and say: This murderer is staying in my room—just dropped in, so to speak. They'd never understand.

General (who doesn't understand either)

Quite.

Prince

They're too stupid!

(The General looks annoyed, but the Prince is too excited to notice.)

General (sourly)

As you say.

Prince

I was a little shocked when he showed up at my home. I was prepared to send him about his business for his presumption, even though I had been considering seeing him. It isn't a good idea, to do that, you know. But, he's such a fine young man, you see— When I heard his story, I could not be angry that he came to me, he has no one else to turn to. Absolutely no one. He has done the right thing. Russia will bless him.

General

May I speak to him?

Prince

Certainly. He's waiting in the next room.

(The Prince goes to the door and returns with Razumov, who enters and bows to the General.)

Prince (presenting Razumov)

General Tulayev, this is the young man I have been speaking of, Mr. Razumov.

General

This is an extraordinary story you tell, Mr. Razumov. But, I wonder if the bird has flown while you were visiting Prince Kropotkin.

Razumov

The door is locked— I have the key in my pocket.

General (surprised)

I see you are a very capable young man. I thought, perhaps, this might be some sort of joke to ingratiate yourself with the Prince. I see it is not. What is this fellow's name?

Razumov

His name is Haldin. Victor Victorovitch Haldin.

General

It may surprise you, but we have heard of him. But, we never thought he was much trouble.— Can you tell me how he was dressed?

Razumov

Blue topcoat. Boots.

General

Hmm. That answers the description. Is he tall or short?

Razumov

Very tall.

General

Hmm. Take a chair, Mr. Razumov. Why are you standing?

Prince

Mr. Razumov is a young man of conspicuous talent. I have it at heart that his future should not—

General

Certainly not. We shall keep him out of this. (to Razumov) Has he any weapons about him?

Razumov

I don't think so. But my kitchen utensils, knives, that sort of thing, are lying about.

General

Good. Precisely. (to the Prince) We want this bird alive. It will be the devil if we can't make him sing a little before we are done with him.

(Silence.)

Razumov (bravely)

I hope that will not happen. I am giving him up to justice, you understand, I—

General

Of course, of course. But we must protect the Tsar— and some eggs must be cracked to make an omelet.— Mr. Razumov understands that, too.

Razumov

Haldin will never speak.

General (grimly)

That remains to be seen.

Razumov

I am certain. A fanatic like that never speaks.— Do you suppose I am here from fear?

General

Certainly not. And I don't mind telling you, if you had not come forward like a good patriot, this monster would have disappeared like a stone in the water. And that would have a detestable effect.

Razumov

He had all but made good his escape. So you see, there can be no suspicion of fear—

Prince

Nobody doubts the moral soundness of your action. Be at ease on that point, young man. Youth is so touchy.

Razumov

Perhaps so—but my comrades at the University will hold that I have betrayed him—and them. It is terribly difficult to do one's duty.

General

That's so, that's true. I understand the situation perfectly.

Prince

And, I venture to insist that my role and that of this patriotic youth not become public. He is a man of promise of great abilities.

General

I haven't a doubt of that. He inspires confidence.— I don't mind saying, I was skeptical until I met him.

Prince

I don't want him to suffer for his patriotism—for doing his duty.

General

Yes, yes, I am thinking it out.— How long is it since you left him at your rooms, Mr. Razumov?

Razumov

About one o'clock.

General

And, you meant to say, he came to you—to take you into his confidence, and to trust you to meet this peasant for him—with no prior acquaintance—with no indication you were in sympathy—?

Prince (quickly)

Whom the gods wish to destroy they first make mad. No doubt, he utterly misunderstood some exchange of ideas—some speculative conversation—

General (wryly)

Mr. Razumov—do you often indulge in speculative conversation?

Razumov

No, Excellency. I am a man of deep convictions—but I generally keep them to myself. They are not popular in the circles I travel in—the student societies. So, I keep my mouth shut. Crude opinions are in the air—but I've never thought them worth combating.

Prince

A serious young man.

General

I see that. Mr. Razumov is quite safe with me. I am interested in him. He has, it seems, the useful quality of inspiring confidence.— But it seems to me, this Haldin could have come to you and simply talked for some hours under any pretext he chose, and thus achieved his objective of finding shelter. Why would he make these revelations unless he sought your assistance?

Razumov

I see what you have in mind—

General

I have nothing in my mind—

Razumov

I believe it is because he is too honest.

General (shocked)

Honest?

Razumov

He is like a child. He wants help, but he would rather die than expose me to any danger under a false pretense. Does that seem strange? Yes, of course it does. That is why I pity him and feel I am betraying him, even though I abhor what he did with all my soul. I provoked no confidence, I asked for no explanations.

General

It's rather a pity that you did not! He seems to be in quite a communicative mood. Do you know what he means to do?

Razumov

He plans to meet a sledge about half an hour before midnight on Kesabelnaya Street. At the Seventh Lamppost.

General

Well! There is a way to keep your protégé quite clear of any connection with the actual arrest. We shall be ready before midnight.

Prince

I will remember this, General Tulayev. I will remember this.

General

I am happy to be able to do a man of your rank such a service, albeit an unusual one.— Half an hour before midnight. Till then we must rely on Mr. Razumov. You don't think he is likely to change his plans?

Razumov

How can I tell? But men like that never do.

General

What men?

Razumov

Fanatics: men who worship liberty like the worshippers of Kali, by committing murder in her name. I detest rebels of every kind. I detest everything he stands for. Yet, I pity him.

General

They shall be destroyed then.

Razumov

He's made a sacrifice of his life already—in his own mind. If Haldin does change his plans, depend upon it, it will not be to save his own life, but to attempt some new outrage. But that is not likely. He's worn out with his exertions.

General (vowing)

They shall be destroyed!

Prince

What a terrible necessity!

General

There's one comfort. This one leaves no posterity. I've always said it—one effort, swift, pitiless, persistent, steady—and we're done with them forever. How I hate them! My life has been built on loyalty. To defend the Tsar I am ready to lay down my life,—yes, and even my honor, if that were needed. But what honor is there in a war against these anarchists and atheists. Brutes! It is horrible to think of.

Prince

This young man is fit to understand your memorable words!

General

I must now ask Mr. Razumov to return to his home. I think he has been away too long. Note that I do not ask him to justify his absence to his guest. I don't ask him to do that. But a longer absence must arouse this criminal's suspicions. I have perfect confidence in you, Mr. Razumov.

Razumov (sourly)

Everyone seems to. I'm not sure it's a good trait.

Prince (arm on his shoulder)

And I have confidence, too.

Razumov

Dear Prince, you have been of aid to me when I most needed it. I should not have presumed had I—

Prince

I understand perfectly, dear boy. Perfectly.

Razumov

I am sure that in the future I will not have cause to trouble you again. Such situations as these do not occur more than once in a lifetime.

Prince

And you have met this one with courage and patriotism. It gives me a high idea of your worth. You have only to persevere—to persevere. I hope you are perfectly at ease now, as to the consequences—

Razumov

After what your Excellency has done for me, I can only rely on my conscience—

Prince

Dear boy. You make me very proud. I will take an interest in you, I promise you—

General

And so will I—

BLACKOUT

ACT I
SCENE 3

The General's office.

The General is seated comfortably in a large armchair. Razumov is shown in by an officer who leaves without saying a word.

Razumov

I haven't lost a moment.

General

Very proper, very proper.

Razumov (furious)

Why was my room searched? I am totally misunderstood—totally.

General

My dear young man, you are mistaken.

Razumov

Is this an official inquiry? Am I suspected of something?

General

This is not strictly official. In fact, I don't want it to have that character at all.

Razumov

Then, why was I officially requested to report here?

General

Oh, the request was official, but we wouldn't have dreamed of enforcing it. It's just our way of doing things.

Razumov

I am a suspect. A suspect!

General

I would have said "misunderstood person."

Razumov

Do I have to endure your satire as well? I know I am only a student—

General

Quite well connected—

Razumov (ignoring this sally)

Allow me the superiority of mind over the unthinking forces that are about to crush me out of existence. I am amazed that the police delayed the search for two days. I could easily have burned any compromising papers.

General

The search was conducted as a matter of form—and for your own good. You are angry? Is that reasonable?

Razumov

I am reasonable—rational, for that matter. I am not an intellectual anarchist. I think like a Russian. I take the liberty to call myself a thinker. It is not forbidden, as far as I know.

General

Not at all, not at all. Why should it be forbidden? Why should it be forbidden? I, too, consider myself a thinker, or at least a thinking man. The idea is to think correctly. Religious belief is a great help.

Razumov

That man—Haldin—believed in God.

General

Really? You tell me more than we were able to get out of him. He was judged by a special commission of three officers. He told us absolutely nothing. (handing over a dossier) Here is the interrogation. After every question: Witness refuses to answer. Page after page. He left me nothing to begin my investigation on.— That is why I want to talk with you in more detail.— The man was a hardened criminal. And you say he believed in God?

Razumov

Blasphemers do.

General

No doubt you had many discussions with him on that subject.

Razumov

Hardly. He talked and I listened. Intently, you may be sure, but that is hardly a conversation.

General

Listening is a great art.

Razumov

And getting people to talk is another.

General

Well, that's difficult, very difficult, except, of course, in special cases. For instance, this Haldin, nothing could induce him to speak.

Razumov

Indeed? I thought you had methods?

General

If I were playing games with you, my dear Razumov, I would pretend he had incriminated you. He didn't.

Razumov

Very nice of him. He ruined my life anyway, or so it seems to me. How dare he come to me like that? You know, he told me he had moved out of his rooms a month before, so his landlady would not be bothered by the police. He seemed to think of everyone's safety but mine!

General

He refused to speak even when your personality was put forward.

Razumov

My personality? I don't understand.

General

It was judged necessary. The case was too serious to leave any stone unturned—you understand that yourself, I am sure. (pause, Razumov is silent) So, it was decided that a certain question should be put to the accused. In deference to the wishes of your—to the wishes of Prince K—your name was not mentioned. Even the judges themselves were kept in ignorance. Your father recognized the propriety, even the necessity of what we proposed. He was concerned for your safety. Things do leak out, but I assure you, every precaution was taken. It was the last question asked. Question: Has the man, well known to you, in whose rooms you remained for several hours on Monday— and on whose information you have been arrested— has he had any previous knowledge of your intention to commit political murder? Prison refuses to reply Question repeated four time with the same results.

Razumov

And if he had answered and cleared me?

General

I am afraid we would have thought he was trying to protect you.

Razumov

Of course. You would think that!

General

A stubborn man, Haldin. He even refused confession from the chaplain. That was the only time he spoke. He was sentenced to death by hanging. Sometimes after that a prisoner will become communicative. Not Haldin.

Razumov

When will the sentence be carried out?

General

It was carried out this morning. We saw no reason to delay the execution. Silent to the last.

Razumov

So quickly. He had a belief in a future life. (rises and starts to leave)

General (surprised)

What are you doing?

Razumov

I will tell you what! You think you are dealing with a secret accomplice of that unhappy man! I hated him. Visionaries work everlasting evil on earth. There is no sentimentality in my hatred of that man. I don't hate him because he committed murder. Anyone can do that. I hate him because I am sane. It is his fanaticism that outrages me—

General

What a tirade!

Razumov

What is his death, or that of the minister, to me? I hardly knew Haldin, and the minister not at all. The intelligentsia get drunk on ideas. We Russians are a drunken lot. Intoxication of some sort we must have. What is a sober man to do in this country? If a drunk runs up and kisses you, and tells you you are his dearest friend, you can break your cane on his head, and not succeed in beating him off.

General

Of course, of course. Kirylo Sidorovitch, calm yourself.

Razumov

Why am I called here to be confronted with his silence?
With his execution? What is his silence to me? This is
incomprehensible.

General

The service you have rendered is appreciated.

Razumov

Is it?

General

And your position, too. But, only think, you fall into
Prince Kropotkin's study, as if from the sky—

Razumov

As Haldin fell in on me.

General

Certainly, certainly. Still, some curiosity is bound to—

Razumov

Naturally you have the right—or should I say the power—

General

I prefer to say the duty—

Razumov

Very well. But, it's all perfectly useless. I told you everything I know. Everything!

General

I told Prince Kropotkin of my intention of becoming personally acquainted with you. He approved.

Razumov

Did he? So, he is suspicious, too? Well, after all, he doesn't know me very well. But it is not exactly my fault!

General

Is it necessary to take it that way, my dear young man?

Your father—

Razumov

Perhaps not. But I do. But there is no appeasing your curiosity or your suspicions. I knew it would be this way. I am probably lucky not to have hanged with Haldin. So be it. I am a patriotic Russian— whether I inherited those instincts or not, I am in no position to say.

General

I have been greatly impressed by your political confession—that was found in your rooms. A very remarkable document. May I ask for what purpose—?

Razumov

Why, to deceive the police, naturally. What is all this mockery? I protest against this comedy of persecution. You have clearly shown me that you still suspect me, and that I have no chance of appealing to my father for protection. Very subtle. I understand. With all due respect, sir, I must claim the right to be done with this man—once and for all. So, (bowing) I take the liberty to retire.

General

Kirylo Sidorovitch—

Razumov (repeating emphatically)

To retire—

General (smiling)

Where to?

(They stare at each other.)

CURTAIN

ACT II
SCENE 4

Some months later in Switzerland.

A small room in a Swiss villa decorated in the Russian fashion. Razumov is in conversation with Peter Ivanovitch, an older revolutionary, and one of the leaders of the conspirators exiled in Switzerland.

Peter

On my word, young man, you are an extraordinary person.

Razumov (disgustedly)

You are mistaken, Peter Ivanovitch. If I were really an extraordinary person, I would not be here with you in Switzerland, Canton of Geneva, Commune of—what's the name of the commune this place belongs to? Never mind—in the heart of democracy, anyhow. A fit heart for it: not very large, and not worth very much. I am no more extraordinary than the rest of us Russians, wandering in foreign parts.

Peter

No! No! You are not ordinary. I have some experience of Russians who are—well—living abroad. You appear to me—and to others, as well, a marked personage.

Razumov (suspiciously)

What do you mean by that?

Peter

You don't suppose, Kirylo Sidorovitch, that I have not heard of you from various points where you made yourself known on your way here? I've had letters.

Razumov

Oh, we're great about talking of each other. Gossip, tales, suspicions, and all that sort of thing, we know how to deal in to perfection. Calumny, even.

Peter

Heavens! What are you talking about? What reason can you have to—?

Razumov

I am talking of the poisonous plants that flourish in the

world of conspirators—like evil mushrooms in a dark cellar.

Peter

You are casting aspersions—which as far as you are concerned—

Razumov

No! I cast no aspersions—but it is just as well to have no illusions—

Peter

The man who says that he has no illusions, has at least that one.— But I see how it is, you aim at stoicism.

Razumov

Stoicism. That's a pose of the Greeks and the Romans. Let's leave stoicism to them. We are Russians, that is to say, children, sincere, cynical if you like. But that's not a pose.

Peter

I'm astonished. Supposing you are right—how can there be any question of gossip or slander in your case? The fact is there is not enough known about you to invent gossip, let alone slander. You are a mystery man.— You have done a great deed. But you have not been communicative. People who have met you have written me—but I form my own opinions. You are a man out of the common. That's positively so. You seem like a man with a secret. You inspire confidence.

Razumov

Spare me.

Peter

You have the airs of Brutus.

Razumov

This is ridiculous. Do you mean to say that revolutionaries are patricians, and that I am, of all things, an aristocrat?

Peter

Not all patricians, though there are some. But you, at any rate, are one of us.

Razumov

To be sure, I am not a democratic Jew? How can I help it? I have no name, I have no—

Peter

But, my dear friend. My dear, Kirylo Sidorovitch—

Razumov

I have no legal right to the name of my father. I don't wish to claim it. I have no father. But I will tell you what: my mother's father was a serf. I don't want anyone to claim me. But Russia cannot disown me. She cannot. I am Russian.

Peter

Hmm! You're proud, aren't you? And, I don't say you have no justification for it. You are one of us. I allude to your birth only because I think it is important.

Razumov

I attach some importance to it, also. I won't even deny that it may have some importance for you, too. But suppose we talk no more of it.

Peter

We shall not. Not after this one time. This shall be the last occasion. You cannot believe for a moment that I had the slightest idea of wounding your feelings. You are clearly a superior nature. Quite above the common susceptibilities. But the fact is, I don't know your susceptibilities. Nobody, outside Russia, knows much of you, as yet!

Razumov

You have been watching me?

Peter

Yes. Two things I may say to you at once. I believe, first of all, that neither a leader nor any decisive action will come out of the people. Everything in a people that is not genuine, not its own by origin or development—is well, dirt. Intelligence in the wrong place is dirt. Foreign bred doctrines are dirt. Dirt! Nothing but dirt!— The second thing I say is this: at this moment there is a chasm between the past and the future— a chasm that can never be bridged by foreign liberalism. Bridged it can never be. It must be filled. Do you understand, enigmatical young man? It has got to be filled up.

Razumov

Don't you think that I have already gone beyond meditation on that subject? A sacrifice of many lives alone is necessary.

Peter

Let's have some tea. (going to a samovar and pouring some tea for Razumov) You don't object to being understood—to being guided?

Razumov

In what sense? Be so good as to understand I am a serious person. What do you take me for?

Peter

You shall know soon enough.

(At this moment, enter Madame, a very well dressed Russian woman of a certain age who begins speaking immediately.)

Madame

Enfin. Vous voilà!

Peter

Yes, here I am. And, I have with me a proven revolutionary—a real one.

Razumov (aside)

A witch, a veritable witch—with a Parisian dressmaker.

Madame

We have been hearing about you for some time. And you know that the general complaint is that you are too reserved.

Razumov (ironically)

I am, don't you see, a man of action.

Madame

You see, Kirylo Sidorovitch, I have been shamefully robbed, (laughing) positively ruined. A slavish nature would find consolation in the fact that the robber was nothing less than a Grand Duke. Do you understand, Mr. Razumov?— No! You have no idea what those people are: downright thieves.

Peter (to Madame)

You will only upset yourself.

Madame

What of that? I say thieves, thieves!

Peter

No power on earth could rob you of your genius.

Razumov (totally at sea)

I really don't understand—

Peter

It's not necessary that you should. If she continues in

this vein she will upset herself.

Madame (raging)

Perfect swindlers—and what base swindlers at that! A family that counts a creature like Catherine the Great in its ancestry—what can you expect of a Romanoff!

Peter

Please calm yourself.

Madame

Oh, very well. (closing her eyes, she stands perfectly rigid) (opening her eyes and addressing Razumov) Well, really! You are very reserved. You haven't said twenty words together.

Razumov

I have been listening, Madame—

Madame

Yes,—you understand me perfectly, I can tell. The discontent must be spiritualized. That's what ordinary revolutionaries never understand— because they are not capable of it. For instance, Peter Ivanovitch brought Mordatiev here last month—you've heard of him. They call him an eagle—a hero—yet he's never done half as much as you have. Never attempted half your work. But talk—oh, does he talk. I have a plan for starting a little something in the Balkans. Do you know what he said to me? "What have we to do with Balkan intrigues? We must simply extirpate the scoundrels."— All very well—but what then? The imbecile! I screamed at him: But you must spiritualize, don't you understand, spiritualize the discontent.

Razumov

Spiritualize—yes, of course.

Madame

An odious creature. Imagine a man who takes five lumps of sugar in his tea. "Yes," I said, "spiritualize. How else can you make the discontent effective and universal?"

Peter

Listen to this, young man. Effective and universal.

Razumov

Some say hunger will do that.

Madame

Yes, I know—but you cannot make famine universal. It is not despair we want to create. There is nothing to be got out of that. What we want is indignation!

Razumov

I am not a Mordatiev.

Madame

Bien sur.

Razumov

Though, I, too, am ready to say extirpate. Or more bluntly—kill them. But, pardon me, Madame, won't a Balkan intrigue take a long time?

Madame

In matters of politics, I am a spiritualist. A supernaturalist.

(Peter Ivanovitch signals Razumov to discontinue the subject.)

Peter

Eleanor!

Madame (disregarding him)

We have plans—

Peter

Eleanor.

Madame

What is it? Ah, yes—the girl.

Razumov

The girl?

Madame

The sister of your friend: Miss Haldin.

Razumov

I do not know her.

Madame

What are you saying? I understand she was here—talking to you—in the garden.

Razumov

Yes, in the garden. She made herself known to me.

Madame

And then ran away from us all—after coming to the very door! What a peculiar proceeding! Well, I was once a shy provincial girl. Yes, that's my origin. A shy provincial family.

Peter

You are a marvel.

Madame (to Razumov)

You must bring that wild thing here. She is wanted. I reckon upon your success.

Razumov

She is not a wild young thing.

Madame

All the same. She may be one of these conceited Marxists. Do you know what I think? I think she is very much like you in character. There's a fire burning in you—and in her, too. (staring at Razumov) I can see your very soul.

Razumov (amused but uneasy)

And what do you see?

Madame

I cannot tell you.

Razumov

I myself once saw a phantom.

Madame

Of a dead person?

Razumov

No—living.

Madame

A friend?

Razumov

No.

Madame

An enemy?

Razumov

I hated him.

Madame

Ah, it was not a woman, then?

Razumov

Why should it have been a woman?

BLACKOUT

ACT II
SCENE 5

The same as Scene 4, but a few weeks later.

Razumov and Peter Ivanovitch are in conversation.

Razumov

I really have no mind to turn into a dilettante spiritualist, or spend my time in spiritual ecstasies, or in the gospel of feminism. I made my way here for my share of action—action! It was not Peter Ivanovitch the writer and literary lion who attracted me. It was an idea. There are men in Russia who believe in you so much that it seems to be the only thing that keeps them alive in their misery. Think of that.— Of course, I don't speak of the people: they are animals.

Peter

Say children.

Razumov

No! Animals!

Peter

They are innocent, they are sound.

Razumov

Animals are sound enough. But give them power and you'll see what they will do. Never mind. Let us pass that subject. There is not a student group in Russia that meets without your name being whispered. Not as a writer, but as the center of the revolution. What else has drawn me, driven me,—yes, driven me to you?

Peter

Ah yes, yes, what else—

Razumov

All these days you have been trying to read me. We Russians are prone to talk too much. I've always felt that. I assure you that I am not likely to talk so much again.— It's absurd of me to talk like this. You must admit, I have not tried to please. But, one thing: I hope to be of use—but a mere blind tool I can never consent to be.

Peter

The moment of action approaches.

Razumov

Sometimes I think you only talk of action.

Peter

Do not be so impatient. (giving Razumov a paper) Read this.

Razumov

Well, this is more in my line.

Peter

Do you accept the mission?

Razumov

Without a question.

Peter

Then, burn that paper as soon as you have understood your instructions. You will not discuss it with me again—or with anyone else. If you have any questions, ask me now.

Razumov (taking the paper to an ashtray and carefully burning it)

I have none. I understand perfectly.

Peter

You must come to see us again. You must bring along Haldin's sister, Nathalie Victorovna.

Razumov (uneasily)

What do you want of her?

Peter

Everyone shall be wanted presently.

Razumov

I do not wish to see her suffer the fate of her brother.

Peter

She has more reason than he to wish the revolution. His act was purely disinterested. She has the additional stimulus of revenge.

Razumov

She's only a woman. A child.

Peter

That is what heroines are made of. Think of Antigone. Of Charlotte Corday.

Razumov

Can she work with me?

Peter

That will have to be decided later. You must excuse me, my friend, I have other work to do. Come again, come again.

(Peter Ivanovitch goes out. Razumov prepares to leave, when Sophia, a kind, plain woman, enters.)

Sophia

What—are you going way? How is that, Razumov?

Razumov

I am going, because I haven't been asked to stay.

Sophia

I have come to bring two gentleman to see Peter Ivanovitch, I've just managed it. Just got in from Zurich.

Razumov

Yes, of course. And they're from Zurich, too?

Sophia

From quite another direction. From a distance, from a distance. From America, in fact. The time is drawing near. I did not tell them who you were. Yakovlitch would have wanted to embrace you.

Razumov (looking out the window)

Is that him, in the long coat?

Sophia

You've guessed it right. That's Yakovlitch.

Razumov

And, they couldn't find their way here without you coming all the way from Zurich to help them? Truly, as Peter Ivanovitch says, without women we can do nothing. So it stands written, and apparently it is so.

Sophia

What is the matter with you?

Razumov

I don't know. Nothing. I've had the devil of a day.

Sophia

What of that? Men are so moody. One day is like another—hard, hard,— and that's always true—until the great day comes. Peter Ivanovitch does not know them. I am the only one at hand that remembers them from the old days. It's natural enough, isn't it?

Razumov

You came to vouch for his identity?

Sophia

Yes, and his character. Fifteen years changes a man. When I think of Yakovlitch before he went to America! We were not in our first youth even then. But a man is always a child.

Razumov

You were lovers with him? Why didn't you follow him to America?

Sophia

Fifteen years ago the revolution was very active. You are in it, but you don't seem to know it. Yakovlitch went to America on a mission. I went back to Russia to carry on the struggle. After the police crackdown there was nothing to come back to. A whole generation had been wiped out.

Razumov

Ah, indeed, nothing!

Sophia

What are you trying to insinuate? Suppose he did get discouraged a little?

Razumov (at the window)

He looks like a Yankee. A regular Uncle Sam. Well, and you? You who went to Russia? You did not get discouraged?

Sophia

Never mind me. Yakovlitch is a man who cannot be doubted. He's got the right stuff.

Razumov

Pardon me, but does that mean you think I don't have the right stuff? (pause) Is it because I don't accept blindly every development, such for instance, as the feminism of our great Peter Ivanovitch? If that is what makes me suspect, then I can only say I scorn to be the slave, even of an idea.

Sophia

No, no—your ideas are probably all right. You may be valuable, very valuable. What's the matter with you is that you don't like us.

Razumov

Am I expected to have love as well as convictions?

Sophia (rounding on him)

You know very well what I mean! People have been thinking you are not quite wholehearted.

Razumov

You are mistaken about that. Your perspicacity is at fault.

Sophia

What phrases he uses! You are like all men: egotistical. You've had no training either. What you want is to be taken in hand by some woman. I am sorry I am not staying or I would attend to it myself. I must go back to Zurich.

Razumov

I am sorry, too. But, all the same, I don't think you understand me.

Sophia

And, how do you get on with Peter Ivanovitch? You seem to have seen a good deal of each other. How is it between you?

Razumov

Well enough. But, I'm not sure where I stand with him.

Sophia

No one is. That's all right.

Razumov

Soon you will see him. He will be curious to know what your impressions are of me.

Sophia

No doubt Peter Ivanovitch will have something to say to me. He is inclined to trust me. What shall I say to him?

Razumov

I don't know. Tell him of your discovery.

Sophia

What's that?

Razumov

Of my lack of love for revolutionaries.

Sophia

Why, that's between ourselves.

Razumov

I see that you want to tell him something in my favor. Well then, tell him I am very much in earnest about my mission. I mean to succeed.

Sophia (surprised)

You have been given a mission?

Razumov

It amounts to that. I have been told to bring about a certain event.

Sophia

What sort of mission?

Razumov

Something in the nature of propaganda work.

Sophia

Ah,—far away from here.

Razumov

No. Not very far.

Sophia

So! Well, I am not asking questions. It is sufficient that Peter Ivanovitch should know what each of us is doing. Everything is bound to come right in the end.

Razumov

You think so?

Sophia

I don't think, young man. I simply believe it.

Razumov

And is it to Peter Ivanovitch that you owe your faith?

Sophia

That's just like a man. As if it were possible to tell how a belief comes to one. One must believe for pity alone. Millions of people in Russia would envy the life of dogs in this country. This cannot go on. No! For twenty years I have been working, looking neither to the right, nor to the left. You are only at the beginning. You have begun well—but you must trample down every particle of your own feelings. You cannot stop. You must work.— Perhaps, you think I am complaining?

Razumov

I don't think anything of the sort.

Sophia

I dare say you don't, you dear superior creature! You don't care.— Men are all alike. You mistake luck for merit. Men and women have been at work constantly for twenty years—looking neither to the right nor to the left.— What's the use of talking. And here two babies come along and succeed in striking a great blow at the first try. Well, I was young once.— What was he like?

Razumov

Who?

Sophia

Haldin. What did he look like?

Razumov

How like a woman. What is the good of concerning yourself with his appearance? He is beyond all feminine influences now.

Sophia

You suffer, Razumov.

Razumov

What nonsense! Formerly the dead were allowed to rest. Perhaps Madame could conjure him up for you— for I take it she is a witch.

Sophia

I hope she'll conjure us up some tea.— But, that is by no means certain. I am tired, Razumov.

Razumov

You tired! What a confession! Well, if you hurry, you may see her, rather than wasting your time with such an unsatisfactory, skeptical person as myself. But, as to your being tired, I can hardly believe it. We are not supposed to be. We mustn't. We cannot. The tireless activities of the revolutionary parties impresses the world. It's our only prestige.

Sophia

Flouts and sneers. And what for, pray? Simply because some of his conventional masculine notions are shocked. One might think you were a neurotic. But, I have just learned something that makes me think you are a man of character. Yes, a strong character.

Razumov

If you don't look out, you will certainly miss seeing so much as the ghost of that tea.

Sophia

Never mind—it will be no great loss. As to the lady, you must understand that she had her positive uses.

Razumov

Money

Sophia

Lots of it.

Razumov

I see.

Sophia

Material must be obtained in some way. And this is easier than breaking into banks. More certain, too.

Razumov

I admire Peter Ivanovitch's self sacrifice. It's enough to make one sick.

Sophia

Squeamish man! Sick! Make him sick! And, what do you know about it? Peter Ivanovitch knew her years ago when they were both young. When a man throws off his squeamishness, a woman is no match for him. But, how seldom. The silliest woman is always useful; because she is never squeamish.— What are you smiling at I should like to know?

Razumov

I am not smiling.

Sophia

Smirking. You made some sort of face.— In life, there is no choice. You either rot or burn. And a woman prefers to burn than rot.

Razumov

Rot or burn! Perfectly stated. Do tell me. She would be infernally jealous of him, wouldn't she?

Sophia

Who? What? The Baroness Eleanor Maximovna jealous of Peter Ivanovitch? Such a thing is not to be thought of.

Razumov

Why? Can't a wealthy old woman be jealous?

Sophia

What put it in your head to ask such a question?

Razumov

Masculine frivolity, if you like.

Sophia

I don't like it. It is not the time to be frivolous.— Or, perhaps, you are only playing a part?

Razumov

Playing a part. It must be done very badly since you see through me so easily.

Sophia

You are mistaken. I am doing no more than the rest of us.

Razumov

Who is doing what?

Sophia

Everybody.

Razumov

You are a materialist, aren't you?

Sophia

Eh! Dear boy, I have outlived that nonsense.

Razumov

But you must remember—I am sure, "Man is a digestive tube."

Sophia

I spit on that—on materialism.

Razumov

What? But, you cannot ignore the importance of good

digestion. The joy of life, you know—the joy of life depends on a sound stomach. Whereas, bad digestion inclines one to skepticism—breeds bleak fancies—thoughts of death. These are facts ascertained by physiologists. I assure you, that ever since I came here from Russia, I have been stuffed with indigestible foreign concoctions of the most nauseating kind—pah!

Sophia

You are joking!

Razumov

Yes, it's all a joke. It's hardly worthwhile talking to a man like me.

Sophia

On the contrary, I think it is worthwhile. Shallow talk is a weakness we must pardon in you.

Razumov

Thanks. I don't ask for mercy. But, aren't you afraid Peter Ivanovitch might suspect us of plotting something unauthorized?

Sophia

No, I am not afraid. You are quite safe from suspicions while you are with me, my dear young man. Peter

Ivanovitch trusts me. He takes my advice. I am his right hand in certain important things. Do you think I am boasting?

Razumov

God forbid! I was only thinking to myself that Peter Ivanovitch seems to have solved the woman question almost completely.

Sophia (archly)

One doesn't know what to think of you, Razumov. You must have bitten something sour in your cradle.

Razumov

Hmm! Something sour? That's an explanation. Only, it was much later.— But we come from the same cradle.

Sophia

Russia? (Razumov nods) Yes. No wonder then. One lies wrapped in evils for swaddling clothes, watched over by beings that are worse than ogres. They must be driven away—destroyed utterly. That's how I came to feel in the end. The great thing is not to quarrel amongst ourselves over conventional trifles. Remember that, Razumov.

Razumov

I'll try my best.

Sophia

Tell me, is it true that one the very morning of the deed, you attended classes at the University?

(Razumov is silent.)

Sophia

I know you are not boastful. One must say that for you. You are a silent, bitter man. You are not an enthusiast. Perhaps, you are the stronger for that. But you might tell me.

Razumov

Certainly, I went to lectures. But, what makes you ask?

Sophia

I had a letter from a young man in Petersburg, one of us, of course. You were seen taking notes.

Razumov (warily)

What of it?

Sophia

I call such calmness superb, that's all. Nobody could have guessed.

Razumov

Oh, no. Nobody could have guessed—because, don't you see, nobody knew at that time—

Sophia

Yes, yes. But, it takes exceptional fortitude. You looked exactly as usual. It was remembered afterwards—with wonder.

Razumov

It cost me no effort.

Sophia

More wonderful still! Your intention was to stay in Russia?

Razumov

I had no plans of any sort.

Sophia

You simply walked away.

Razumov

Simply, yes. The snow was coming down very thick, you know. It was simple enough. I turned into a narrow side street. I felt inclined to lie down and go to sleep.

Sophia

Right there?

Razumov

Right there. But I went home. Straight to my rooms.

Sophia

You dared?

Razumov

Why not? I assure you, I was perfectly calm. Calmer than I am now, perhaps.

Sophia

And, nobody in the house saw you return?

Razumov

No one. The landlady was out. The cleaning girl out back, I think. Fate? Luck? What do you think?

Sophia

I just see it! And then?

Razumov

I looked at my watch, since you want to know. There was just time. I ran, I flew downstairs. Where would a student be running if not to his classes. At night it's another matter. It's best not to be seen or heard. The people that are neither seen nor heard are the lucky ones in Russia! Don't you admire my luck?

Sophia

Astonishing. If you have luck as well as determination, then indeed, you are likely to turn out an invaluable acquisition for the work at hand. And yet, Razumov, you have not the face of a lucky man.— I suppose it was agreed beforehand that once the business was over, each of you would go his own way?

Razumov

Was that not the best thing? We did not give much thought to what would come after. We never discussed, formally, any line of conduct. It was understood.

Sophia

But, to stay in Russia?

Razumov

It was the only safe course for me. Moreover, I had nowhere else to go. Actually, if Haldin had gone about his business as I did, I don't believe he would have been taken.

Sophia

Yes, yes. You don't know what this wonderful Haldin intended? Perhaps, he might wish to get in touch with you?

Razumov (shrugging helplessly)

I stayed home the next day. You are aware, I suppose, that I was not seen the next day at lectures.

Sophia

I see. It must have been trying enough.

Razumov

You seem to understand one's feelings. It was trying. It was horrible. It was an atrocious day. It was not the last.

Sophia

Yes, I understand. Afterwards, when you heard they had got him. It's like losing a brother. One is ashamed to be a survivor. And, I can remember so many. Never mind! They will be avenged soon. And besides, what is death? It is not a shameful thing, like some kinds of life.

Razumov

Some kinds of life—

Sophia

Life, Razumov, not to be vile, must be a revolt—a pitiless protest— all the time. You understand me, Razumov. You are not an enthusiast, but there is an immense force of hate in you. I feel it. Directly I set eyes on you, back in Berlin, I felt it. You are full of bitterness—and that is good. Love of one's fellow man flags sometimes; but an uncompromising sense of hate, a sense of necessity and justice armed you to strike down that fanatical brute—for it was nothing but that! It could have been nothing but that!

Razumov

I can't speak for the dead, but as for myself, I can assure you that my conduct was dictated by necessity and by the sense—well, of retributive justice. No pity.

Sophia

Listen to my story, Razumov. My father was a working man. He protested his wages and he was knouted by the Cossacks. I was still a child. But from that moment, I was a revolutionary. I was sixteen when I went to the secret societies. I went as soon as I knew how to find my way. And look at my white hair. There's a lot of it. I had magnificent hair, even when I was a chit of a girl. Only in those days, we cut it short in protest. It was a first step towards crushing the infamy. A fine watch-word.

Razumov

You are eloquent, Sophia Antonovna. Only so far, you seem to have been writing in water.

Sophia

Who knows? Very soon, it may become a fact written all over that great land of ours. And then one will have lived long enough. White hair won't matter.— We shall not meet again very soon, I think. I am leaving tomorrow.

Razumov

For Zurich?

Sophia

Yes, and perhaps farther on, after that. When I think of all my journeys, the last must come someday.

CURTAIN

ACT III

SCENE 6

Peter Ivanovitch's room in Madame's villa.

Sophia Antonovna and Yakovlitch, a man known only as N. N. and Razumov. Sophia is presenting Razumov.

Sophia

This is Razumov.

N. N.

Oh, yes! Razumov. We have been hearing of nothing but Mr. Razumov for months. For my part, I would rather see Mr. Haldin on this spot than Mr. Razumov.

Razumov (angrily)

What's the meaning of this?

Sophia

Tut! N. N.—that's what we call him, he had no other

name, just initials—is always like that.

N. N.

What now? What now? I am only sincere. It is not denied that Haldin was the leading spirit. I am not a sentimentalist. It would have been better if Haldin had been spared to us. I say what I think.

Sophia (to Razumov)

Pay no attention to him. It's his way of dramatizing himself.

Razumov

Don't concern yourself. (laughing) Don't mention it. (suddenly serious) Enough of this! I will have no more of it. I can see what you are at with these allusions. Inquire—investigate! I defy you. I will not be played with—I won't have it.

Sophia

Calm yourself, Razumov. What is the matter with you? Don't shout. (to N. N. and Yakovlitch) Go away. Leave him to me.

(Yakovlitch and N. N. go out.)

Sophia

Take care, Razumov. If you go on like this, you will go mad. You are angry with everybody—and with yourself—and on the look out for something to torment yourself with.

Razumov

It's intolerable. You must admit I can have no illusions as to the attitude with which I am regarded. It is only too clear.

Sophia (getting water)

A glass is water is what you want. It's you, my dear, who are flinging yourself at something which does not exist. What is it? Self reproach or what? It's absurd. You were under no duty to give yourself up because your comrade was taken. On the contrary.

Razumov

Apparently, I was under such a duty. Why else does everyone look on me with such suspicion?

Sophia

No one—no one has been shown so much confidence from the very first.

Razumov

It would be rude, but I feel like laughing in your face.

Sophia

You will soon be given an opportunity to show your devotion.— As to what remains obscure in the fate of poor Haldin—well, I have a bit of intelligence. You remember the letter I spoke of?

Razumov

The letter? Perfectly. Some busybody was reporting my conduct on a certain day. No doubt the secret police are greatly edified when they open and read these interesting and superfluous letters.

Sophia

The Okhrana does not get hold of our letters so easily as you imagine—or as easily as they would like. This was hand carried to England for mailing.

Razumov

I'm impressed.

Sophia

The writer relates an incident that may be connected with Haldin. I intended to tell you when N. N. and

Yakovlitch came along.

Razumov

That was also an incident of a very charming kind.

Sophia (losing patience)

Leave off that! Nobody cares for N. N.'s barking. There's no malice in him.

Razumov

No malice? Why he's murdered several people!

Sophia

Spies, by order of the Central Committee.— Listen to what I have to say. There was a peasant in Petersburg who owned houses—he was not an ordinary man of his class. He lived in a brothel.— Did Haldin ever speak to you of that house?

Razumov

Yes. He mentioned it to me once. He used to visit some workmen there.

Sophia

Exactly. In a stable.

Razumov

No doubt. It was probably the cleanest spot in the whole house.

Sophia

The driver associated with burglars. Some of them got captured, and it is suggested that they gave information to the police.

Razumov

About what?

Sophia

Did your friend ever mention a certain Ziemianitch?

Razumov

To be sure. It was one of the last conversations we had together.

Sophia

Shortly before—?

Razumov

How could it have been after?

Sophia

And he spoke of him favorably?

Razumov

With enthusiasm—as a free spirit. Haldin was inclined to take unexpected fancies to people—on insufficient grounds.

Sophia

There! That settles it. The suspicions of my correspondent were aroused.

Razumov

By this Ziemianitch? Probably a drunkard.

Sophia

You talk as if you knew him.

Razumov

No. But I knew Haldin.

Sophia

I see. Well, this Ziemianitch was found dead one morning—hanging from a hook in the stable. Do you begin to see?

Razumov

Some of them end like that. What is your idea?

Sophia

Remorse. He was a Judas. Your friend had a plan to save himself—at least to get out of Petersburg. And that fellow with his horses were part of the plan.

Razumov

It's possible. It's possible.

Sophia (intuitively)

I'm sure of it. He may have betrayed Haldin deliberately or through indiscretion—who can tell? A man like that would be capable of anything.

Razumov

Haldin, in any event, misplaced his trust.

Sophia

It is right now to make this evidence generally known. I have it in my pocket now.

Razumov

Tell me, please. Was this investigation ordered?

Sophia

No, no. There you go again with your sensitivity. Don't you see, there was nothing to investigate? A perfect blank. That's why people were receiving you cautiously. It was all so mysterious—

Razumov

A pious person would say the hand of God has done it all.

Sophia

My poor father would have said that. Not that his God ever helped him or the people. Anyway, it's done.

Razumov

All this would be quite final, if there was any certitude that Haldin was the person who associated with this Ziemianitch.

Sophia

Oh, that's certain. My correspondent was very familiar with his appearance.

Razumov

If that is so—

Sophia

The creature has done justice on himself.

Razumov

What? Ah, yes! Remorse.

Sophia

Don't be harsh. He was a man of the people. The simple Russian soul is never completely impenitent. It's something to know that.

Razumov

Consoling.

Sophia

Leave off railing! Women, children, and revolutionaries hate irony—it negates all faith. Don't rail! Leave off—I don't know how it is, but there are moments when you are abhorrent to me.

Razumov

There are moments when I am abhorrent to myself.

Sophia

Don't mind me—

Razumov

I don't mind. I rather like you.

Sophia

Do you know Ziemianitch thought the devil was after him? A young man in a black coat had beaten him while he was dead drunk in the stable?

Razumov

The devil?

Sophia

The actual devil.

Razumov

But you, Sophia Antonovna, you don't believe in the veritable devil?

Sophia

Do you? Not that we don't have men worse than devils in Russia.

Razumov

And, this dark young man—

Sophia

Never seen before or afterwards.— Why are you smiling, Razumov?

Razumov

At the devil being young after all these ages. But, how was he able to describe him, if he was dead drunk at the time?

Sophia

Oh, the Madame saw him.

Razumov

Does she believe it was the devil, too?

Sophia

Who knows. What's your opinion?

Razumov

Some police hound in disguise. Who else would beat a helpless man so unmercifully?

Sophia

Who indeed? Well, I am going. But first, I will talk to Peter Ivanovitch. Good luck, young man.

(Sophia Antonovna goes out. After a moment N. N. comes in. Razumov and N. N. stare at each other.)

N. N. (after assuring himself that they are alone)

You are succeeding wonderfully, Razumov. You have even convinced Sophia Antonovna.

Razumov

What do you mean?

N. N.

She's completely taken in. And, she is the key to everything. (pause) General Tulayev has ordered me to tell you that your father died recently and has left you a substantial legacy. You are indeed fortunate.

Razumov

Yes, this is a day of wonders.

BLACKOUT

ACT III

SCENE 7

A sitting room in the Haldin residence.

Nathalie Haldin comes in with Sophia Antonovna from the street.

Nathalie

Will you come in for a moment?

Sophia

It's too late.

Nathalie

You know my mother likes you so much.

Sophia

I will just come in to hear how your mother is.

Nathalie

I don't know how I will explain to her that I could not find Mr. Razumov She has taken it into her head that I am concealing something from her. You may be able to persuade her.

Sophia

Your mother may mistrust me, too.

Nathalie

You! She respects you terribly.

Sophia

I am going. I have work to do.

Nathalie

You always have work.

Sophia

We're revolutionaries. Tell your mother I hope she is better.

(Sophia Antonovna leaves. Nathalie looks around and after a moment, Razumov enters from an inner room.)

Razumov

Good evening, Miss Haldin.

Nathalie

Mr. Razumov, I have been looking for you everywhere.

Razumov

Perhaps you are surprised at this late hour. But, you see, I remembered our conversation. I thought it was really your wish—and your mother's wish that I should—so I came. No other reason. Simply to tell—to tell what I have heard myself only today.

Nathalie

Yes, yes—I am very grateful to you for coming at once—like this. Only, I wish I had— Did mother tell you?

Razumov

I wonder what she could tell me that I didn't always know?

Nathalie

What is it that you always knew?

Razumov

If it had not been for a word of greeting or two, I would doubt whether your mother was aware of my presence, you understand?

Nathalie

Yes. Isn't it heartbreaking? She has not shed a tear— not a single tear.

Razumov

Not a tear! And you, Nathalie Victorovna, have you been able to cry?

Nathalie

I have. I am young enough to believe in the future. But, when I see my mother so terribly distracted, I almost forget everything. I ask myself whether I should feel proud or only resigned.— Many people have presented their respects—utter strangers. It was impossible to keep our door shut. There was much sympathy, but some exulted openly at my brother's death. But it isn't worth it. It isn't worth the price she is paying for it. I thought that you were the only person who could assist me.

Razumov

In comforting a bereaved mother? But, there is a question of fitness— has that occurred to you?

Nathalie

Why? Who more fit than you?

Razumov

Indeed! Even before seeing me. It is another proof of that confidence which—never mind. Men are poor creatures, Nathalie Victorovna. They have no intuition. To speak fittingly to a mother who has lost her son, a man must have some experience of the filial relation. It is not the case with me. That does not mean I am insensible—

Nathalie (warmly)

I am certain your heart is not unfeeling.

Razumov

No. My heart is not as hard as stone. No, not so hard. But, how to prove what you give me credit for—ah!— that's another matter. No one has asked such a thing of me before. No one whom my tenderness would have been any use to. And now, you come. You! Now! No, Nathalie Victorovna—it's too late. You must expect nothing from me.

Nathalie

What do you mean?

Razumov

You have given yourself up to illusions while I have managed to remain in the reality of life—our Russian life.

Nathalie

A cruel reality.

Razumov

And ugly. Don't forget that. Very ugly. Look where you like. Look near you—look back at home. Ugly. All the same.

Nathalie

One must look beyond the present.

Razumov

The blind can do that best. I have had the misfortune to be born clear-sighted. And, if you only knew what strange things I have seen. What amazing and unexpected apparitions! But, why talk of all this?

Nathalie

On the contrary, I want to talk of all this with you. Yes, with you especially. With you of all the people in the world. It is in you that we can find all that is left of his generous soul. We are unable to give up our beloved dead. (Razumov makes a hasty gesture of leaving) You are going?

Razumov

I? Where to? Yes, I am going. But, I must tell you first—a story. A story that I heard this afternoon.

Nathalie

I know the story already.

Razumov

You know it? Have you correspondents in St. Petersburg also?

Nathalie

No, no. I head it from Sophia Antonovna.

Razumov

I told your mother most of it. She has not shed a tear. She no longer belongs to this world.

Nathalie

You don't know how bad it had come to be. She expects to see him.— It will end by her seeing him.

Razumov

Hmm! That's very possible. I wonder what—

Nathalie

That would be the end. Her mind will be gone, and then her spirit will follow.

Razumov

You think so? No! There's neither truth nor consolation to be got from phantoms of the dead. I intended to tell her something true—that your brother meant to save his life—to escape. There can be no doubt of that. But, I didn't tell her.

Nathalie

You didn't! But, why?

Razumov

I don't know. Other thoughts came into my head. You were not there. I made up my mind never to see you again.

Nathalie

For what reason?

Razumov

I think that I refrained from telling your mother from—prudence. Yes, from prudence. I might have told her that he mentioned you both.

Nathalie

Some day you must.

Razumov

He was with me.— He said that you had trustful eyes. Why I have not been able to forget that phrase, I don't know. He meant that you have no guile, no deception—that there is nothing in your heart that could give you a conception of a living, acting, speaking lie—if it ever came in your way. You are a predestined victim. That's a distasteful thought. You don't understand? Why should you? Very well, so you talked with Sophia Antonovna?

Nathalie

Yes—she spoke very highly of you.

Razumov

Did she? Things are going well, then. Everything conspires in my favor.— You know Peter Ivanovitch intends to get hold of you?

Nathalie

Get hold of me?

Razumov

Turn you into one of his inspired feminist revolutionary automatons. To carry on your brother's work, I am sure. Does the idea appeal to you?

Nathalie

I really don't know.

Razumov

You know, Nathalie Victorovna, I have the greatest difficulty in avoiding belief in a special Providence. It's irresistible. Or the devil, perhaps. But if so, he had overdone it altogether—that Old Father of Lies—our national patron, our domestic god—whom we take with us when we venture abroad.

Nathalie

What is it, Kirylo Sidorovitch? Why are you looking

at me like this? I have approached you frankly. But, now that you have come to us in your kindness—you alarm me. You speak in riddles. It seems as if you were keeping something from me.

Razumov

Indeed, everything about you is beautiful, Nathalie Victorovna. I wish I could know the innermost depths of your soul, your feelings—

Nathalie

That is kind of you—

Razumov

Have no fear. It is not to betray you. Tell me—do you believe in remorse?

Nathalie

What a question!

Razumov

You are right. What can you know of it? It is not a person like you— What I meant to ask is do you believe remorse can be effective?

Nathalie (sincerely)

Yes.

Razumov

Then, the man who betrayed your brother was redeemed—absolved—by hanging himself?

Nathalie

Yes.

Razumov

Still—he was a brute.

Nathalie

A man of the people.

Razumov

And the people must be forgiven. That's what Peter Ivanovitch says.

Nathalie

We must all be forgiven.— You are concealing something from me.

Razumov

Do you also believe in a duty of revenge?

Nathalie

The future will be merciful to us all. Revolutionaries and reactionaries—betrayers and betrayed. They shall all be pitied. Pitied and forgotten.

Razumov

No revenge for you, then? Never? Not the least bit? Strange—that does not make it easier.— Do you know why I came to see you?

Nathalie

Something troubles your soul.

Razumov

It is simply because there was no one else in the whole world I could go to. Do you understand what I say? No one to go to. Do you conceive the desolation of the thought—no one to go to? An hour after I first saw you, I knew how it would be. The terrors of remorse, revenge—are like nothing to the terrors—to the atrocious temptation you put before me.

Nathalie (becoming excited)

Explain to me, explain to me what you mean!

Razumov

There is no more to tell. It ends on this very spot.

Nathalie (very disturbed)

It is impossible to be more unhappy. It is impossible. I feel my heart is like ice.

Razumov

The most trusting eyes in the world your brother said of you—when he was as good as a dead man. And, when you stood before me the other day, with your hand extended, I remembered the very sound of his voice. But, don't be deceived—I believed that I had in my breast nothing but an inexhaustible hatred for you both.

Nathalie (quietly)

Why?

Razumov

Because he looked to you as the perpetuation of his life. He! The man who robbed me in an instant of my hardworking, purposeful existence. I, too, had my guiding idea— But enough of that. Hate or no hate, when I saw you, I knew I could never drive away your image. This is his revenge. He haunts me in you. You were appointed to undo the evil by making me betray myself back into truth and peace. You! And, you have done it in the same way in which he ruined me—by forcing upon me your confidence. Only what I found detestable in him, in you I find noble.— But don't be deceived. I have suffered from as many vipers in my heart— Listen—now comes the true confession. The other was nothing. Just the beginning. Your brother had stolen my life— I had nothing else in this world— and he was living on through you. And do you know what I said to myself? I WILL STEAL HIS SISTER'S SOUL! Yes, I thought by speaking to me of her trustful eyes he himself has delivered her into my hands.— If you could have looked into my heart you would have cried out with terror—with horror. Perhaps you don't believe such baseness is possible? I was possessed. I gloated over the idea. And then, this poor Ziemianitch hanged himself—as if to help me further my plans for crime. The strength of falsehood seemed irresistible. You could not suspect me.— I saw you were defenseless. It saved me, your innocence. I began to feel that I loved you. And to tell you that, I must first confess. Confess, and then perish. You have freed me from hate. I suffer horribly—but I am not in despair. In giving your brother up, it was myself, after all, whom I betrayed most basely. You must believe what I say now— You cannot refuse to believe this. I simply lack the courage to be either a good man or a scoundrel.

(Nathalie gestures toward him without saying a word.)

CURTAIN

EPILOGUE
SCENE 8

A bleak deserted park. It is winter but no snow has fallen. Trees are barren. General Tulayev sits on a bench reading a newspaper. From time to time he looks at his watch. Precisely as a distant Church bell rings N. N. approaches and stops before the General.

N. N.

I am on time?

General

To the minute. You were not followed?

N. N.

No. They trust me. Especially after the exposure of Mr. Razumov.

General

How did that come about?

N. N.

I believe he fell in love with Haldin's sister. She's quite attractive. He confessed to her.

General

Did she expose him?

N. N.

No, she said nothing. But apparently confessing to one person was not enough for him. At a meeting we had a few nights later he took it upon himself to exonerate Ziemianitch, because suspicion had fallen on him as Haldin's betrayer.

General

What folly! He was lucky he wasn't killed on the spot.

N. N.

After such an orgy of sincerity he obviously was harmless. But several of the comrades were indignant and inflicted a beating on him. As a result of the beating he was rendered deaf.

General (looking piercingly at N. N.)

I heard it was you who did that. You know the trick of bursting ear drums.

N. N. (after a brief silence, quite nonchalantly)

After that he ran out into the street and was almost immediately struck by a motor vehicle.

General

It was not Mr. Razumov's lucky day.

N. N.

He couldn't hear the car approach. He is a horrible cripple and stone deaf at that.

General (after a pause)

What else?

N. N.

Several things. Miss Haldin is returning to Russia.

General

On a mission?

N. N.

Not so far as I can tell. She wants to do volunteer work among the poor.

General

She'll be carefully watched. What else?

N. N.

Peter Ivanovitch stands to inherit Madame's fortune when she dies. And she's very ill.

General

We know that.

N. N.

If we could prevent it?

General

How?

N. N.

By either destroying her will, or better yet forging one.

General

Then that nest of vipers would be left without funds. That's an idea I like. Can you manage it?

N. N.

Of course. But I'd expect to be well rewarded.

General

Of course. We must talk about this in detail.

N. N.

It would be convenient if Madame were to die as soon as the forgery is prepared.

(The General nods. They walk off together.)

CURTAIN

ABOUT THE AUTHOR

Frank J. Morlock has written and translated many plays since retiring from the legal profession in 1992. His translations have also appeared on Project Gutenberg, the Alexandre Dumas Père web page, Literature in the Age of Napoléon, Infinite Artistries. com, and Munsey's (formerly Blackmask). In 2006 he received an award from the North American Jules Verne Society for his translations of Verne's plays. He lives and works in México.

www.ingramcontent.com/pod-product-compliance
Lightning Source LLC
LaVergne TN
LVHW091308080426
835510LV00007B/416